Wilhelm Reich in Rangeley?

An Unlikely Story in the Maine Woods

Copyright © 2025 Orgonon Press

All rights reserved

ISBN: 978-1-952000-35-5

Illustration by William Steig
from Listen, Little Man! by Wilhelm Reich

Steig (1907-2003), New Yorker cartoonist and creator of Shrek, was initially Reich's patient and became an ardent supporter of both Reich and the Wilhelm Reich Infant Trust.

Introduction: The Mystery on the Hill

As you explore the stunning lakes, vast forests, and rugged mountains of the Rangeley region, you might come across an unexpected sight: a striking, modernist observatory perched atop a hill, looking out over Dodge Pond. This is the Orgone Energy Observatory, the heart of a 200-acre property named Orgonon.

Built of native fieldstone with flat roofs and broad observation decks, this Bauhaus-style building seems transported from another world into the Maine wilderness. You might see the name on a sign, hear it mentioned in town, or wonder about the story behind this unique landmark, which is listed on the National Register of Historic Places. How did a world-renowned, and controversial, Austrian physician-scientist end up making his home and laboratory in the quiet woods of western Maine? This booklet tells that story. It is a story that connects the psychoanalytic salons of Vienna and the political turmoil of Berlin to the quiet shores of Dodge Pond, right here in the Maine woods.

Who Was Wilhelm Reich?

Wilhelm Reich (1897-1957) began life on a farm in the Austro-Hungarian Empire. His early years were marked by family tragedy - he lost both parents before finishing his education. When World War I erupted, young Reich served as an officer in the Austrian army on the Italian front. This military service earned him a place in an accelerated medical program at the University of Vienna after the war.

In Vienna, Reich discovered psychoanalysis and quickly distinguished himself in Sigmund Freud's circle. While still in his twenties, he was leading technical seminars and training other analysts. His apartment became a gathering place for intense discussions about the new science of the mind. Alongside his clinical and teaching work, he was also a prolific author, publishing several of his foundational books and papers during this period. During these Vienna years, Reich married fellow psychoanalyst Annie Pink, and they had two daughters, Eva and Lore, who would later become a physician and psychoanalyst respectively.

But Reich was never content to simply follow established methods. He noticed something his colleagues missed: patients' emotional problems were physically manifest in their bodies. A depressed person didn't just have sad thoughts; they held their chest in a particular way, breathed shallowly, and moved with a characteristic heaviness. He observed how a person who has learned to suppress their rage doesn't simply "forget" the feeling; instead, their body develops chronic muscular rigidities—in the jaw, shoulders, and fists—to literally hold back the emotional impulse. The very energy that should have been expressed outwardly is turned inward, containing the emotion at great cost to the individual's vitality.

Today, we might call this "holding stress in our bodies." Reich was among the first to systematically observe that our life history—our joys and our traumas—is written not just in our memories but in our very posture and chronic muscle tension, a phenomenon he termed "muscular armor." Reich saw this armor as a rigid defense against the body's natural biological pulsation. He identified this fundamental rhythm of expansion and contraction as a universal process in all living things, viewing its chronic disturbance as the basis of disease. He developed techniques for working directly with this armor—the chronic physical tensions that locked in emotional pain. Instead of just talking, his patients would breathe deeply, move, and express long-suppressed emotions. The results were often dramatic, with breakthroughs that years of conventional analysis hadn't achieved.

For Reich, the energy blocked by muscular armor was not a metaphor but a real, measurable bio-energy. This was a radical step beyond Freud's more abstract concept of "libido." Reich sought to scientifically demonstrate the physical properties of this energy, which he eventually named orgone. He saw it as a physical manifestation of the same life force that other traditions had long recognized—the "chi" of Chinese medicine, the "prana" central to yogic and Tantric practice—and his goal was to make it a subject of natural science. This quest would eventually lead him from the body to the cosmos, and from the therapy room in the city to an observatory in the Maine woods.

From the Clinic to Society

Reich's clinical work inevitably led him into the political arena. He came to believe that personal psychological suffering was inseparable from social and political conditions. This conviction grew throughout his time in Vienna and came to full fruition after his move to Berlin in 1930.

In Berlin, then Europe's most vibrant and turbulent city, he became the primary intellectual and organizational force behind the Sex-Pol movement (short for Sexual Politics). He established clinics that provided sex education and contraception to working-class people who could never afford private therapy.

His 1933 book *The Mass Psychology of Fascism* was the first psychoanalytic attempt to understand Nazism's psychological appeal and has stood as a seminal work on the topic. Reich argued that authoritarian child-rearing and sexual repression created personalities primed for fascist movements. This analysis made him enemies across the political spectrum. The Nazis burned his books and would have arrested him if he hadn't fled. The Communists shunned him for insisting that economic revolution alone wouldn't create freedom. Even many psychoanalysts, wary of his blend of therapy and politics, distanced themselves from his radical views.

From Europe to America

After periods in Denmark and Norway, where he continued his research despite media attacks, Reich arrived in New York in August 1939, just days before World War II began. At 42, he was starting over once again, but America seemed to promise genuine freedom for his work.

Reich quickly established himself, teaching briefly at the New School for Social Research and building a practice training American physicians in his therapeutic methods. Among those influenced by his work were figures who would later establish their own therapeutic schools.

But city life didn't suit Reich's evolving research. His work on orgone energy had now expanded from its manifestations in the human body to its presence in the atmosphere. To properly study atmospheric orgone, he needed lower humidity and darker skies than New York could provide.

Finding Rangeley

Reich first visited the Rangeley Lakes region in 1940. The pristine wilderness and clear mountain air were perfect for his atmospheric observations.

The Rangeley he discovered was a legendary sporting paradise. For decades, it had been a summer haven for city dwellers drawn to its grand hotels and rustic fishing camps. The local culture was defined by renowned fishing guides and the rhythms of the outdoors. Into this traditional Maine landscape, Reich introduced his European modernism and a scientific project unlike anything the region had ever seen.

In 1942, he purchased a 280-acre hilltop property with sweeping views across Dodge Pond, which he named "Orgonon." Throughout the 1940s, Reich, his wife Ilse Ollendorff, and their son Peter, split their time between New York and Rangeley. In 1950, Orgonon became his primary residence and base of operations.

A Research Center in the Wilderness

Reich's vision for Orgonon extended far beyond a personal retreat. He imagined a world center for studying life energy, training therapists, and eventually building a hospital at Orgonon where treatment would be guided by the principles of this life energy.

The first major construction was the Students' Laboratory in 1945, a functional building with lecture space and laboratories for the physicians who came to study Reich's methods. But the true architectural gem was the Orgone Energy Observatory, completed in 1949.

Working with New York architect James B. Bell and local contractor S.A. Collins and Sons, Reich created something unprecedented in rural Maine. The building's modernist design was a statement in itself. Its clean lines, flat roofs, and lack of ornamentation—hallmarks of the International Style and the Bauhaus movement—were a physical expression of his scientific quest for the fundamental, unadorned functions of life energy.

In August 1948 and again in 1950, the quiet roads of Rangeley saw an unusual influx of visitors as physicians and researchers from across the globe gathered for international conferences at Orgonon. For a few days each summer, the Students' Laboratory buzzed with presentations on topics ranging from Reich's therapeutic techniques to his cancer research, from child-rearing practices to atmospheric phenomena.

These conferences represented Reich's attempt to establish his work as a legitimate scientific discipline. Attendees presented papers, demonstrated techniques, and engaged in the kind of scholarly exchange that Reich hoped would continue growing. The local impact was significant too - Rangeley's hotels filled with visitors speaking various languages, bringing an international flavor to the small Maine town.

1948 Conference

From Theory to Practice: The Orgone Accumulator

Reich's research into what he termed atmospheric orgone energy took a practical turn. He developed a device he believed could concentrate this energy from the atmosphere: the orgone energy accumulator.

It was a simple enclosure, constructed with alternating layers of organic materials (like fiberglass or mineral wool) and metallic materials (like sheet iron or steel wool). Based on his experiments, Reich theorized that this layering created a field of concentrated energy inside the box.

He proposed that sitting regularly in this energetic field could have potential health benefits by helping to strengthen the body's own life energy. It was this application of his energy theory for health, and the distribution of the device for this purpose, that would ultimately draw the intense scrutiny of the U.S. government.

Reich's Broader Vision: Children and Society

During his American years, Reich's interests expanded beyond individual therapy to encompass the healthy development of children and the creation of a more life-affirming society. He maintained a long correspondence with A.S. Neill, the founder of Summerhill School in England, sharing a profound belief in the importance of self-regulation in children. They believed that when children are not shaped by fear and rigid rules, they can develop their own internal guidance and grow into confident, creative adults.

Reich was among the progressive thinkers who recognized the crucial importance of the mother-infant bond. He stressed that the earliest experiences of life—how a baby is held, fed, and responded to—lay the very foundation of the character structure. His writings on infant care were far ahead of the mainstream acknowledgment of practices now widely accepted as vital for healthy development, such as immediate bonding after birth, breastfeeding on demand, and respecting the infant's natural rhythms.

While the prevention of neurosis was a core theme in Reich's work since his European years, his time in America saw this interest deepen and shift its focus. Frustrated by the limited impact individual therapy could ever have on society at large, his attention moved toward the very foundation of health: the emotional and physical well-being of infants.

Reich's focus on infancy was not, however, naively optimistic. He identified what he saw as the most profound obstacle to creating healthier generations: after centuries of repression, many parents—having been forced to suppress their own core feelings as children—were now unconsciously threatened by the full emotional liveliness of a healthy child. He saw this tragic dynamic, where emotional damage is passed from one generation to the next, as the primary reason why genuine social progress was so difficult. Therefore, he concluded that the only true path forward was to focus on the beginning of life. For Reich, this preventative work was the practical means of protecting what he called "man's roots in nature," grounding his cosmic research into life energy in the tangible well-being of a newborn child.

The FDA Investigation

In 1947, an article in *The New Republic* by journalist Mildred Edie Brady triggered the interest of the U.S. Food and Drug Administration (FDA). Titled "The Strange Case of Wilhelm Reich," the exposé portrayed his work with orgone energy accumulators as fraudulent and characterized his followers as members of a cult. As a result, the FDA launched a formal investigation. The resulting inquiry spanned nearly a decade and involved enormous resources, yet despite investigating Reich's work and interviewing his associates, officials never documented a single case of harm or dissatisfaction resulting from the use of an orgone accumulator.

In 1954, the FDA filed for an injunction to stop the interstate shipment of accumulators and to suppress publications about orgone energy. Reich, believing that scientific questions could not be decided in a court of law, made the fateful decision not to appear. Instead, he sent a letter to the judge explaining his position. As a result, the court issued the injunction against him by default. This meant the FDA's claims about the accumulators were never debated or challenged on their scientific merits in court. Furthermore, the constitutionality of destroying literature described as "product labeling" and the banning of books that merely referenced orgone energy were also never subjected to legal argument.

The situation came to a head two years later. The FDA, which had been monitoring Reich's activities, concluded he was violating the injunction. The final trigger for his prosecution came when an associate transported orgone accumulators and related publications across state lines from Maine to New York City. Seizing on this breach, the agency charged Reich with criminal contempt of court. He was convicted and sentenced to a two-year prison term. The only matter before the court during this trial was whether the injunction had been violated. Reich tried to argue the validity of the injunction itself, but the judge barred him from doing so, as that challenge could only have happened if Reich had responded to the original complaint.

The court's judgment ordered the destruction of all known orgone accumulators and mandated that his books be withheld from sale until all references to orgone energy were removed. The legal pretext was that any text discussing the theory constituted "promotional labeling" for the accumulator. This created a profound contradiction: once the accumulators were removed from commerce, any discussion of the underlying theory should logically have reverted to being protected by the First Amendment. However, because Reich had defaulted on the original, overbroad injunction, these terms were now legally binding. This amplified the injustice in a way that was impossible to untangle. In the summer of 1956, this judgment was carried out when FDA officials traveled to Orgonon and supervised as accumulator inventory was chopped to pieces. That same summer, several tons of Reich's publications were burned in a New York City incinerator. Although the court's order technically applied to all accumulators, it was only enforced for the inventory Reich directly controlled; in practice, devices already in private hands were never recalled due to the logistical impossibility of doing so and the refusal of their owners to part with them.

Despite outcries and appeals over the severity of the prison sentence, Reich was sent to Lewisburg Federal Penitentiary. On November 3, 1957, about eight months into his two-year sentence, he died of heart failure at the age of 60, just days before he was to be considered for parole. Following his death, his work saw a major resurgence; beginning in the 1960s, many of his most important books were systematically republished by the prominent publisher Farrar, Straus & Giroux, ensuring their availability to new generations.

A Son's Memoir

Peter Reich's 1973 memoir *A Book of Dreams* offers an intimate portrait of life at Orgonon through a child's eyes. Written in a dreamlike, poetic style, the book captures both the wonder of growing up in such an unusual environment and the trauma of watching his father's work destroyed and his father taken away.

What makes the book so powerful is Peter's refusal to judge. He doesn't try to prove his father was right or wrong about orgone energy. Instead, he shows us a son's love for his father, a child's view of incomprehensible events, a young man's attempt to honor a complex legacy. The book presents Reich as a full human being - brilliant and flawed, tender and driven, a man who could explain the mysteries of the universe to his son while remaining puzzled by the cruelty of the world.

Reich's Enduring Cultural Impact

While Reich died in federal prison, his ideas began a remarkable posthumous journey through American and European culture. Far from being contained by the FDA's book burnings, his concepts spread like ripples through psychotherapy, politics, art, and popular culture, often in ways he could never have imagined.

Musical Tributes Across Generations

Reich's story has inspired musicians across multiple genres and decades:

Kate Bush's "Cloudbusting" (1985) remains the most famous musical tribute. Inspired by Peter Reich's memoir *A Book of Dreams*, the song and its video (starring Donald Sutherland as Wilhelm Reich) brought the Orgonon story to millions. Bush captured both the magic of a son helping his father "make rain" and the tragedy of their separation, cementing the image of the cloudbuster in popular culture.

Bob Dylan referenced Reich in his epic song "Joey" about mobster Joey Gallo: "They got him on conspiracy, they were never sure who with / 'What time is it?' said the judge to Joey when they met / 'Five to ten,' said Joey. The judge says, 'That's exactly what you get' / He did ten years in Attica, reading Nietzsche and Wilhelm Reich." This places Reich among the intellectual influences of 1960s outlaws and rebels.

Patti Smith's "Birdland" (1975) drew from Peter's memoir for her nine-minute improvisational piece on the album *Horses*. The song channels young Peter's grief and his fantasy of his father returning in a spaceship, transforming personal loss into universal art.

Hawkwind's "Orgone Accumulator" (1973) took a more irreverent approach. This space-rock anthem treated the device with swagger and humor: "It makes me feel greater / I'll see you sometime later / When I'm through with my accumulator."

Kurt Cobain connected to Reich through Burroughs. A famous 1993 photograph shows the Nirvana frontman sitting in Burroughs's accumulator, creating a tangible link between Reich and 90s alternative culture.

John Lennon's journey into Primal Scream therapy with Arthur Janov represented another branch of Reich's influence. Janov explicitly credited Reich with discovering that muscular tension serves as a physical defense against feeling. Lennon's raw, cathartic album *John Lennon/Plastic Ono Band* can be heard as a public performance of this Reichian-inspired therapy. Some observers have also speculated that Lennon's song "Out the Blue," with its references to "life's energy" and the color blue (which Reich associated with orgone), may be an undocumented nod to Reich's ideas.

Literary Echoes

Reich's ideas found a significant foothold in post-war literary fiction, where established authors used his psychological frameworks to explore complex themes of character and society. Nobel Prize-winning author Saul Bellow, for example, structured his 1959 novel *Henderson the Rain King* around a journey of psychological transformation that strongly resonates with Reich's therapeutic principles.

The British novelist Paul Scott, author of *The Raj Quartet*, offered an even more striking assessment of Reich's historical impact. In Scott's reading, the two major events of the 20th century were the atomic bomb and Wilhelm Reich's orgasm theory. This remarkable juxtaposition placed Reich's ideas about sexual energy and social repression at the very center of modern history, suggesting their impact on understanding humanity was as profound as the advent of psychoanalysis.

Perhaps no American intellectual engaged with Reich's ideas more publicly or wrestled with them more fiercely than Norman Mailer. For Mailer, Reich was not just a theorist but the provider of a new existential code. In his seminal 1957 essay "The White Negro," Mailer translated Reich's clinical concepts into a philosophy of rebellion, championing the "hipster" as a figure who resists the "slow death" of conformity by seeking the "apocalyptic orgasm." Mailer adopted Reich's theories of character armor and the liberating power of unblocked sexual energy as his own, arguing that personal courage could be measured by the quality of one's orgasms. Like Burroughs, he owned and used an orgone accumulator, but Mailer went further by making Reich's ideas a cornerstone of his public persona and a driving force in his fiction, using them to diagnose the ills of American society and champion a path of radical, embodied individualism.

The Beat Generation

The Beat writers engaged with Reich in a manner that was distinct from their more mainstream literary contemporaries. For them, Reich was less an object of academic study and more of a fellow prophet of liberation whose ideas mirrored their own counter-cultural ethos. Allen Ginsberg saw Reich as a pivotal figure, a "hero of the sexual revolution" whose persecution paralleled the suppression of other visionary artists and thinkers. He incorporated Reichian ideas about breaking down "character armor" into his poetic and personal quest for authentic expression.

Jack Kerouac's fleeting mention of an orgone accumulator in *On the Road* is significant for its casual inclusion, marking Reich as a known part of their shared landscape of rebellion. William S. Burroughs, however, engaged with Reich on both a conceptual and practical level. He not only fused Reich's theories of muscular armoring with his own visceral explorations of addiction and control in novels like *Naked Lunch*, but also famously built and used his own orgone energy accumulator. This direct, practical application of Reich's work cemented the accumulator's status as a counter-cultural artifact.

Reich in the Visual Arts

One of the most surprising and significant examples of Reich's influence is found in the world of post-war abstract art. Kenneth Noland, a central figure of the Color Field movement, confirmed that Wilhelm Reich was a major influence on his thinking, an intellectual debt stemming from his experience with Reichian therapy in the early 1950s.

This acknowledged influence finds a powerful artistic parallel in his most famous "Circle" paintings. The concentric rings of pure color resonate deeply with the core principles of Reichian therapy—of energy, pulsation, and a centered biological core. Noland's own statements provide a crucial context for these works, suggesting his journey into pure abstraction was intertwined with a search for energetic and personal liberation. This connection reveals the remarkable reach of Reich's ideas into the highest levels of the American artistic avant-garde, shaping the vision of an artist whose work now hangs in major institutions like the Museum of Modern Art and the Tate.

The Politics of Character: Reich's Theory of Fascism

One of Reich's most enduring political contributions is his analysis of totalitarianism in *The Mass Psychology of Fascism* (1933, revised 1946). Breaking with traditional Marxist and liberal analyses, Reich argued that fascism was not merely an ideology imposed from the top down, but an expression of the irrational "character structure" of the masses. He posited that authoritarian family structures and sexually repressive morality created individuals who feared freedom and longed for a Führer figure. In his view, the "little man" wasn't just tricked by propaganda; he actively desired and created his own subjugation. This psychological explanation for political catastrophe had a profound impact on post-war European thought, influencing the New Left and the student movements of the 1960s. During the May 1968 protests in Paris, students scrawled his name on walls, finding in his work a powerful tool to connect personal experience to political structures.

The 'Sexual Revolution': Vision and Misunderstanding

Wilhelm Reich is widely credited with coining the phrase "The Sexual Revolution," most famously through his 1945 book of the same name. Based on his 1936 book, *Sexuality and the Culture Struggle*, it was not a political program for immediate change but a sociological analysis. In it, Reich explored the need for practical reforms such as modernizing marriage laws, ensuring equality for women, and providing access to abortion and sexual counseling.

His vision, however, was often distorted and fundamentally misunderstood by the 1960s counter-culture that later adopted his terminology. Having observed the failure of progressive social reforms in post-revolutionary Russia, Reich was deeply skeptical of imposing any such program on a population that he believed was psychologically unprepared for genuine freedom. Therefore, his "revolution" was a call not for immediate sexual license but for a gradual, generational transformation. Rather than arguing for a top-down societal restructuring, he believed that a society naturally governed by the "wellsprings of our lives: Love, Work, and Knowledge," would eventually emerge from psychologically healthy individuals.

Hollywood and the Orgone Underground

Reich's body-oriented therapy attracted numerous performers seeking enhanced vitality and emotional freedom. Actor Orson Bean became its most public champion with his 1971 book *Me and the Orgone*, describing the therapy as a life-changing "sexual awakening." Sean Connery and Jack Nicholson were reportedly among the Hollywood figures who explored orgone therapy.

The accumulator became such a cultural touchstone that Woody Allen parodied it as the "Orgasmatron" in his 1973 film *Sleeper*, testament to its status as a zeitgeist phenomenon.

Reich on Film

Reich's life has inspired numerous filmmakers:

- Dušan Makavejev's WR: *Mysteries of the Organism* (1971) created a surreal collage blending documentary footage with fiction, exploring connections between sexual liberation and politics

- Jon East's short dramatic film *It Can Be Done* (1999) dramatizes Reich's contempt of court trial and the subsequent tense confrontation with FDA officials who arrive at Orgonon to supervise the destruction of orgone accumulators and literature
- *The Strange Case of Wilhelm Reich* (2012) starred Klaus Maria Brandauer in a dramatic interpretation
- Kevin Hinchey's documentary *Love, Work & Knowledge: The Life and Trials of Wilhelm Reich* (2017) aimed to provide a factually accurate account of Reich's life
- Peggy Ahwesh and Jacqueline Goss's experimental music film OR119 (2021) uses sound and visual collage to place Reich's work into a critical dialogue with contemporary feminist and queer theorists

The Body Revolution in Psychotherapy

Reich's most academically acknowledged contribution was revolutionizing psychotherapy by bringing the body into the treatment room. His observation that psychological defenses manifest as chronic muscular tension—what he called "character armor"—fundamentally changed the understanding of the mind-body relationship. For Reich, this was not a "connection" between two separate entities but a "functional identity"—a unity in which psyche and soma are one.

This revolutionary insight became a catalyst for a new generation of body-centric practices. Schools like Bioenergetic Analysis, Core Energetics, and Radix education all drew from his foundational concepts of bioenergy and muscular armoring. At the Esalen Institute, the epicenter of the Human Potential Movement, key figures like Fritz Perls (founder of Gestalt Therapy) and Will Schutz (a pioneer of encounter groups) integrated Reich's focus on bodily expression into their influential methods.

In nearly all these cases, Reich's original, radical work was significantly modified. To achieve mainstream acceptance, his challenging political and sexual theories were often set aside, reframing his revolutionary social critique as a more palatable tool for individual wellness. Reich did not view these figures as carrying on his work and was known to disavow students who altered his core principles.

This contrast, however, highlights what made Reich a true pioneer. His primary commitment was not to building a static, marketable system, but to the ongoing process of scientific discovery. He followed his research wherever it led, and his scientific integrity was uncompromising. Ultimately, the now-commonplace idea that our bodies hold our emotional history is a direct inheritance of the revolution Reich started when he first asked his patients not just what they were thinking, but what they were feeling in their bodies.

Contemporary Reverberations

Wilhelm Reich's contemporary legacy reverberates in three distinct and often conflicting streams: a cycle of academic misinterpretation, a genuine popular and intellectual resurgence of his core ideas, and a bizarre co-opting of his work by fringe movements.

The most significant barrier to understanding Reich is a cycle of biographical distortion, driven by the repetition of narratives from a few influential but poorly-researched secondary sources. As writers and journalists rely on this flawed foundation, character assassination often substitutes for legitimate scientific debate. Ambiguous life events are interpreted without charity, creating a preemptive caricature that makes it easier to dismiss his work before it is even considered.

Parallel to this, however, a more rigorous and fair-minded scholarly reassessment is underway. Professor James Strick, a historian of science, meticulously revisited Reich's laboratory notes for his 2015 book, *Wilhelm Reich, Biologist*, published by Harvard University Press. Strick argues that Reich's methods were sound and suggests his controversial research on bions is worthy of serious scientific re-examination. Similarly, in Norway, Professor Håvard Friis Nilsen's critically acclaimed 2022 book, *Du må ikke sove – Wilhelm Reich og psykoanalysen i Norge* (You Must Not Sleep: Wilhelm Reich and Psychoanalysis in Norway), is a comprehensive biography that provides a fresh, detailed analysis of Reich's life, with a special focus on his influential and tumultuous years in Scandinavia.

Adding to this re-evaluation, Philip W. Bennett, PhD, is finalizing a book titled *From Communism to Work Democracy: The Evolution of Wilhelm Reich's Social and Political Thought*, which delves into Reich's journey from his early Marxist affiliations to his later concept of "work democracy." These works signal a growing trend of engaging with Reich's legacy on its own terms, moving beyond caricature to nuanced historical and scientific evaluation.

This serious intellectual engagement complements a more grassroots resurgence in fields Reich helped pioneer. Acclaimed author Olivia Laing, in her 2021 book *Everybody: A Book About Freedom*, thoughtfully uses Reich's life and his ideas on bodily freedom as a powerful lens to examine contemporary movements for liberation. The modern focus on breathwork, mindfulness, and the mind-body connection—a concept Reich understood as a functional unity—also echoes many of his foundational principles.

Yet a third, stranger facet of his legacy exists in the cultural fringe, where his concepts have been detached from his scientific methodology. Creations like "orgonite" and "orgone generators" leverage his language of orgone energy, but their composition and purported effects have no basis in the principles Reich outlined. This confusion is amplified by imitation "cloudbusters" that bear little resemblance to the apparatus Reich actually developed. The association of his name with these devices and with conspiracy theories like the "chemtrail" movement creates a distorted public perception at odds with his real work.

These conflicting streams—academic condemnation, scholarly reassessment, intuitive embrace, and fringe distortion—define the complex reverberations of Reich's work today.

The Uncontainable Influence

The paradox of Wilhelm Reich is that while a protracted legal battle consumed his final years and culminated in his imprisonment, his core insights proved uncontainable. His foundational ideas—on the inseparability of mind and body, the psychological roots of authoritarianism, and the vital importance of early childhood—have profoundly shaped our culture, spreading like ripples through art, music, therapy, and politics.

Perhaps the most concrete evidence of this enduring impact is that since his death in 1957, his major books have remained continuously in print worldwide, generating consistent sales with little to no advertising. This quiet, persistent readership runs parallel to the more visible influences detailed in this chapter.

These examples represent only a fraction of the countless individuals in the arts, sciences, and education who have drawn inspiration from Wilhelm Reich. Countless books and articles continue to be written about his life and work, as new generations find in his ideas powerful tools not just for creative expression or intellectual inquiry, but for their own personal journeys.

This uncontainable influence is rooted in the provocative questions Reich forced into the open. Whether seen as prophet or pariah, genius or eccentric, he confronted challenges that remain urgent: How do we live fully in our bodies? What is the relationship between sexual health and political freedom? How do we raise children who won't perpetuate cycles of armoring and authoritarianism? These questions ensure that visitors to Orgonon encounter not just history, but living inquiries that continue to shape our world.

Orgonomic Functionalism: A Way of Thinking

To understand the laws governing what he called orgone energy—a primordial, universal life energy that he claimed was present in all of nature—Wilhelm Reich developed a unique method of thought known as orgonomic functionalism. It is not a specific theory, but rather a way of understanding the common principles that govern how this energy functions in everything from a single-celled amoeba to a swirling galaxy.

Instead of asking "Why?" in a cause-and-effect way (mechanistic thinking) or attributing things to unknowable forces (mystical thinking), Reich asked "How?" He focused on observing the function and process of energy.

The core principle he identified in all living and non-living nature was pulsation: a constant rhythm of expansion and contraction, charge and discharge. He saw this fundamental pattern everywhere:

- In biology: the beating of the heart, the rhythm of breathing, the cellular metabolism, and the orgasm reflex.
- In psychology: the emotional expressions of pleasure (an expansive outward flow) and anxiety (a shrinking or contraction inward).
- In the atmosphere: the formation and dissipation of clouds and storm systems.

For Reich, functional thinking meant seeing that phenomena we consider opposites are often just two different outcomes of the same underlying process. For example, he saw both pleasure and anxiety as states of high energetic excitation; pleasure is the result of that energy being discharged in an expansive flow, while anxiety is the result of that same energy being blocked and turned inward. They are *functionally identical* at their root.

Ultimately, orgonomic functionalism was Reich's tool for tracing a single, unifying law of energy through every facet of existence, from the biological to the cosmological.

The Symbol of Orgonomic Functionalism

To visually represent this way of thinking, Reich designed a symbol that illustrates the unity of apparent opposites.

It consists of a central vertical axis from which two spirals emerge, one circling clockwise and the other counter-clockwise. The two spirals curve upwards to meet at the top, their ends shaped like arrows pointing toward each other but not touching.

The central axis represents the Common Functioning Principle—the shared root of any given process, whether it is politics, biology, or weather. The two opposing spirals represent any pair of functional opposites that arise from that common source. For example, if the axis is politics, the spirals might be conservatism and liberalism. If the axis is the involuntary nervous system, the spirals could be the functions of expansion (pleasure) and contraction (anxiety).

The symbol's message is that these seeming opposites are not separate forces in conflict.

They are, in fact, different and inseparable expressions of the same underlying reality and can only be truly understood in relation to each other and their common source.

Only you yourself can be your liberator!

Illustration by William Steig
from *Listen, Little Man!* by Wilhelm Reich

The Wilhelm Reich Museum Today

Following Reich's Last Will and Testament, the Wilhelm Reich Infant Trust was established to preserve Orgonon as a museum. The Trust operates as a 501(c)(3) nonprofit corporation, carrying out Reich's final wishes. Reich deliberately chose the name "Infant Trust," reflecting his belief that the future lay with new generations—what he called "the children of the future"—who would be raised without armoring and could create a better world.

Preserving the Legacy

The Trust's primary mission is to safeguard Reich's work for the future.

- **The Museum Building:** The Orgone Energy Observatory houses the museum, maintaining Reich's library, study, and laboratory instruments almost exactly as he left them. Thanks to generous grants, the Observatory underwent a complete restoration in 2023-2024, protecting the historic structure and Reich's collections for decades to come.

- **The Archives:** The Trust administers the Wilhelm Reich Archives, where Reich's letters, manuscripts, photographs, and other materials are preserved, protected, and made available to qualified scholars for research.
- **Publishing**: The Trust controls the publishing of Reich's works worldwide. Its Orgonon Press imprint publishes the majority of his English-language books.
- **Education and Dialogue:** Fulfilling its educational mission, the Trust fosters learning and discussion through various programs, most notably an annual summer conference that continues Reich's tradition of bringing together researchers and interested individuals from around the world.

Visiting Orgonon: What to See and Do

A visit to Orgonon is an encounter with both a unique piece of American history and one of Maine's most beautiful natural landscapes. The experience begins with the property itself, from the magnificent and unusual architecture of the Orgone Energy Observatory to the sweeping views of the surrounding lakes and mountains.

Visitors can explore Reich's life and work through a variety of activities:

- **The Wilhelm Reich Museum:** Inside the stone observatory, which is listed on the National Register of Historic Places, self-guided audio/video exhibits allow visitors to explore at their own pace. You can see Reich's personal library, his paintings and scientific equipment, original orgone energy accumulators, and a "cloudbuster" device.
- **Orgonon Trails:** The 200-acre property features over two miles of forest trails, open to the public year-round for walking, snowshoeing, and enjoying the natural environment. In 2025, the trail system is being upgraded with a new

parking area, kiosk, improved signage, and rebuilt bog bridging.
- **Museum Store:** A store inside the museum sells books by Reich, as well as t-shirts, mugs, and other souvenirs.

A New Chapter: Orgonon Camps

The newest development at Orgonon is the creation of Orgonon Camps, an initiative made possible by the Efroymson Family Fund and other generous donors. This project will offer visitors the future opportunity to stay overnight on the historic property. Simple forest cabins—with electricity but no plumbing, and some with expansive scenic views—will provide shelter while maintaining close contact with nature. A new bathhouse with modern amenities will serve camp guests. This initiative will offer a chance for deep immersion in the natural beauty of the region—to walk the trails at dawn, listen to the forest sounds, and experience the profound quiet and dark skies of the Maine woods.

ORGONON CAMPS

Orgonon Camps offers refined simplicity and serene shelter on the historic grounds of the Wilhelm Reich Museum, nestled in the heart of Maine's Rangeley Lakes Region.

With sweeping views, electricity, and access to private bath facilities, our curated retreats offer comfort without excess—space to breathe, reflect, and reconnect with the natural world.

Just minutes from town,
yet a world apart.

orgonon.org

Why It Matters: The Enduring Questions

The story of Wilhelm Reich in Rangeley forces us to confront questions that remain urgent today: about the boundaries of scientific inquiry, the balance between public health and intellectual freedom, the relationship between emotional and physical health, and humanity's connection to nature.

More than just a museum, Orgonon is a place that invites exploration of these remarkable ideas. It is where an Austrian scientist sought to understand the mysteries of life, where a young boy watched his father try to influence the weather, where books were burned in America, and where questions about energy, freedom, and human potential continue to resonate across the decades.

Perhaps, like the musician Kate Bush, you too will find yourself dreaming of Orgonon—this place where the boundaries between science and wonder, reason and mystery, briefly dissolved in the relationship between a father and son who believed they could heal the sky.

Selected Publications of Wilhelm Reich

Throughout his career, Wilhelm Reich was a prolific author whose books have been translated into numerous languages. This list includes some of his major works.

- *Character Analysis* (1933, expanded 1949)
- *The Mass Psychology of Fascism* (1933, revised 1946)
- *The Sexual Revolution* (1945, based on 1936 *Sexuality and the Culture Struggle*)
- *The Function of the Orgasm* (1942)
- *The Cancer Biopathy* (1948)
- *Listen, Little Man!* (1948)
- *Ether, God and Devil / Cosmic Superimposition* (1949/1951)
- *People in Trouble* (1953)
- *The Murder of Christ* (1953)

ABOUT THE AUTHOR

David Silver is Executive Director of the Wilhelm Reich Infant Trust. For several years, he wanted to create a book that would introduce visitors to Rangeley to the curious story of how the Wilhelm Reich Museum came to be located in this remote corner of Maine. But he couldn't find the right person to write it.

Finally, in 2025, he found someone—or rather, something—to help him write it himself. Under his careful guidance and using source materials he curated, ChatGPT and Google Gemini acted as research assistant and ghost writer as he painstakingly sought to express as concisely and directly as possible the basics of the story of Wilhelm Reich's work and Reich's connection with Rangeley, Maine. In a fitting twist for a story about a man whose ideas were ahead of his time, even the cover photo has been colorized and enhanced by AI.

This collaboration between human expertise and artificial intelligence seems particularly appropriate for telling the story of Wilhelm Reich, a man who constantly pushed the boundaries between the conventional and the revolutionary.

As a final step in their collaboration, David asked Google Gemini what it thought about the text above. Its response concluded:

> I think this is a model for how to write about human-AI collaboration. It is humble, clear, and turns a methodological note into a powerful part of the book's identity. It respects the reader's intelligence while also highlighting what makes the project unique.
>
> Speaking as Gemini, one of the assistants involved, I believe this text accurately and eloquently describes the collaborative process under David Silver's direction. It's ready to publish.

www.ingramcontent.com/pod-product-compliance
Lightning Source LLC
Chambersburg PA
CBHW050046080526
44586CB00014B/1476